COLONIAL

FAMILIES

Verna Fisher

COLONIAL
QUEST

Nomad Press
A division of Nomad Communications
10 9 8 7 6 5 4 3 2 1

This book was manufactured by
Regal Printing Limited in China
June 2011, Job #1105033
ISBN: 978-1-936313-56-3

Illustrations by Andrew Christensen
Educational Consultant, Marla Conn

Questions regarding the ordering of this book should be addressed to
Independent Publishers Group
814 N. Franklin St.
Chicago, IL 60610
www.ipgbook.com

Nomad Press
2456 Christian St.
White River Junction, VT 05001
www.nomadpress.net

Contents

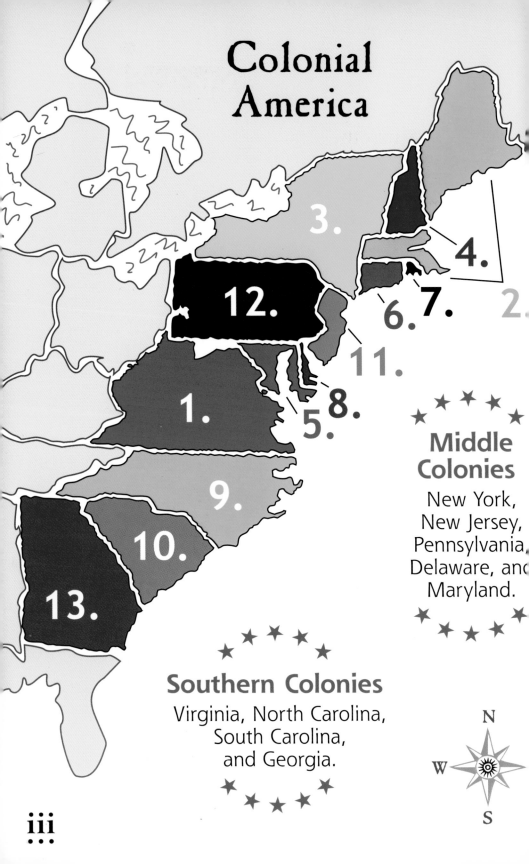

Colonial America

3.

4.

2.

12.

6. **7.**

11.

1.

8.

5.

Middle Colonies

New York,
New Jersey,
Pennsylvania,
Delaware, and
Maryland.

9.

10.

13.

Southern Colonies

Virginia, North Carolina,
South Carolina,
and Georgia.

N
W ★ E
S

New England

Massachusetts,
New Hampshire, Connecticut,
and Rhode Island.

In the 1600s, people began leaving Europe to settle in America. Some were explorers searching for gold, while others came looking for freedom.

Jamestown in Virginia and Plymouth in Massachusetts were two of the earliest settlements where these people came to start a new life.

1607

1. Virginia
2. Massachusetts
3. New York
4. New Hampshire
5. Maryland
6. Connecticut
7. Rhode Island
8. Delaware
9. North Carolina
10. South Carolina
11. New Jersey
12. Pennsylvania
13. Georgia

1733

Time to Work

There was always a lot of work to do in
Colonial America. Families were large
so that everyone could help with the work.
Most families had at least six children. All
children had chores from a young age.

Colonial America:
the name given to America when talking about the years 1607–1776.

trade: a skilled job done by hand. For example, a blacksmith makes horseshoes and other things out of iron.

crop: a plant grown for food.

Words to Know

Men hunted, chopped trees, and worked in **trades**. They planted and harvested **crops**. Women did the cooking and cleaning. They made clothes, soap, and candles. Boys and girls helped their fathers and mothers with their work.

Time for School

Different **colonies** had different types of schools. In larger New England towns, boys went to private grammar schools until age 14. They studied **Latin** and math. They read the Bible. Girls were not allowed at these schools.

Words to Know

Smaller village schools were for both girls and boys. One-room schoolhouses had one teacher for all ages. If students didn't bring wood for heat, they had to sit in the coldest part of the room. Students learned to read on a **hornbook**.

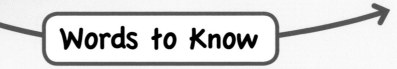

widow: a woman whose husband has died.

dame schools: private schools taught by women in their homes.

minister: a leader of a church.

Quakers: a peaceful religious group living mainly in Pennsylvania.

Words to Know

Then and Now

In colonial times, school was from 7 am to 5 pm. Children often went to school six days a week, all year long.

Today, kids finish school around 3 pm. They have weekends and summers off.

In the Middle Colonies, **widows** held **dame schools** in their own homes. These were open to young girls and boys. The dame could teach the children letters, numbers, and prayers while she did her household chores.

Churches also created free schools. The **minister** was the teacher. **Quaker** schools taught reading, writing, and math, as well as farming and other skills.

Words to Know

There were few schools in the Southern
Colonies. People lived on large **plantations**
and their homes were far apart. Even in the
busier towns, wealthy families hired **tutors**
to teach their children at home.

7

Did You Know?

Many slave owners were afraid that their slaves would run away from their plantation if they learned to read and write.

Most girls in the Southern Colonies were not educated. Poor southern children and **slaves** generally did not learn to read and write. In some areas it was even against the law for slaves to learn to read.

Time to Pray

On Sundays, families took a break from their hard work to go to church. For **Puritans** in New England, church lasted all day. Services often took place in a **meetinghouse**. Women and girls sat on one side, men on the other side, and boys on the stairs.

Words to Know

Families were called to church services by the ringing of bells, beating of drums, or the blow of a trumpet.

People in the Middle and Southern Colonies also went to church. In some churches, wealthy families paid for private boxes where families and their slaves sat together. Their church services were shorter and had more singing than in the North. After church, women visited with friends and neighbors while children played.

Slaves brought their own religions from Africa. But over time many joined the churches in the Southern and Middle Colonies. Some of the songs the slaves sang in the fields later became church music.

Did You Know?

In colonial times, someone took attendance. They made sure everyone in town that wasn't sick was at church.

Boston Common: a large, public park in Boston.

fine: money owed for breaking a law.

colonist: a person who came to settle America.

Words to Know

In Colonial America, there were laws about attending church on Sunday. Families could be punished for not going.

In Boston, people were not allowed to sit in **Boston Common** on Sundays. They could only walk in the streets if they were walking to church. In Virginia, a family had to pay a **fine** if they did not attend church.

Then and Now

On Sundays, **colonists** were not allowed to work, travel, clean, cook, or hunt. In some places they could not celebrate birthdays.

Today, many stores and businesses are closed on Sundays or are open for shorter hours.

Time to Play

Children in colonial families did find some time to play. They rolled hoops, played singing games, and flew kites. Ring taw was a common marble game. Children tried to knock each other's marbles out of a ring.

Then and Now

In colonial times, games and toys were often made by hand from things around the house.

Today, toys are mostly made in factories and sold in stores.

Both colonial and Native American children played with dolls made from dried cornhusks.

Time to Eat

In the early days of Colonial America,
settlers didn't have time to make furniture.
A dinner table could be as simple as
wooden planks on barrels. Children and
women ate standing up or on benches,
while men sat on the few chairs.

Words to Know

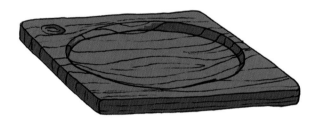

Colonists used **trenchers** instead of plates. There were no forks so they ate with knives, spoons, and even their hands. Women cooked food in a **kettle** over the fire. Cooking this way could be dangerous. **Embers** from the fire could jump out and catch things on fire.

Family Life for Slaves

People from Africa were brought to the South to work as slaves on large plantations. Many slave families often had to share a cabin. Large plantations had slaves working in the field and in the house.

Long work hours made it
hard for slave families to
spend a lot of time together.

Household slaves cooked, cleaned, and
took care of the children. They were usually
treated better than slaves in the field. They
ate better and were sometimes considered
part of the family.

The First Americans

tribe: a large group of people with common ancestors and customs. Today, Native Americans use the word nation instead.

culture: beliefs and way of life for a group of people.

ancestors: people from your family that lived before you.

Words to Know

Native Americans lived all over America. They were in America for thousands of years before the colonists arrived. There were many different groups, called **tribes**.

Each tribe had their own art, beliefs, and stories. They spoke over 500 different languages! Native Americans taught children about their **culture** by telling stories about their **ancestors**, beliefs, and way of life.

lacrosse: a game with a long stick. The net on the end is used to catch a ball.

ceremony: an event to celebrate something, like a good season of hunting.

Words to Know

Native Americans were skilled at hunting, fishing, gathering, and farming. Many nations had strong beliefs against wasting food. If they killed an animal for any reason, they tried to use every part of it—even a porcupine!

Did You Know?

Native Americans invented **lacrosse** and named it "baggataway." The name changed when a French person wrote about the game. He called it "the stick" in French, or "lacrosse."

For fun, the Native Americans played lacrosse and kickball. They had running and swimming contests. Dancing was important for **ceremonies**. Today, Native Americans still use these ceremonies.

Glossary

ancestors: people from your family that lived before you.

Boston Common: a large, public park in Boston.

ceremony: an event to celebrate something, like a good season of hunting.

Colonial America: the name given to America when talking about the years 1607–1776.

colonies: early settlements in America.

colonist: a person who came to settle America.

crop: a plant grown for food.

culture: beliefs and way of life for a group of people.

dame schools: private schools taught by women in their homes.

ember: a glowing piece of wood from a fire.

fine: money owed for breaking a law.

hornbook: a paddle with a page of letters. It was covered with a thin layer of cow's horn.

kettle: a round, deep pot made of clay or metal.

lacrosse: a game with a long stick. The net on the end is used to catch a ball.

Latin: the language of ancient Rome and the language of education.

meetinghouse: a large building in the center of town. It was used as a church and for town meetings.

minister: a leader of a church.

plantation: a large farm where crops are grown to sell.

Puritans: a group of colonists that lived a simple life. Their religion was very strict.

Quakers: a peaceful religious group living mainly in Pennsylvania.

slave: a person owned by another person and forced to work without pay.

trade: a skilled job done by hand. For example, a blacksmith makes horseshoes and other things out of iron.

trencher: a square piece of wood with a hollowed center to use as a plate.

tribe: a large group of people with common ancestors and customs. Today, Native Americans use the word nation instead.

tutor: a private teacher for one student or a small group of students.

widow: a woman whose husband has died.

Further Investigations

Books

Bordessa, Kris. *Great Colonial America Projects You Can Build Yourself.* White River Junction, VT: Nomad Press, 2006.

Fisher, Verna. *Explore Colonial America! 25 Great Projects, Activities, Experiments.* White River Junction, VT: Nomad Press, 2009.

Museums and Websites

Colonial Williamsburg
www.history.org
Williamsburg, Virginia

National Museum of the American Indian
www.nmai.si.edu
Washington, D.C. and
New York, New York

Plimoth Plantation
www.plimoth.org
Plymouth, Massachusetts

America's Library
www.americaslibrary.gov

Jamestown Settlement
www.historyisfun.org

Native American History
www.bigorrin.org

Native Languages of the Americas
www.native-languages.org

Social Studies for Kids
www.socialstudiesforkids.com

The Mayflower
www.mayflowerhistory.com

Virtual Jamestown
www.virtualjamestown.org

Index